CHRISTMAS PIANO SOLOS

ISBN 978-1-4234-5693-3

EXCLUSIVELY DISTRIBUTED BY

Visit Hal Leonard Online at
www.halleonard.com

Contact us:
Hal Leonard
7777 West Bluemound Road
Milwaukee, WI 53213
Email: info@halleonard.com

In Europe, contact:
Hal Leonard Europe Limited
Distribution Centre, Newmarket Road
Bury St Edmunds, Suffolk, IP33 3YB
Email: info@halleonardeurope.com

In Australia, contact:
Hal Leonard Australia Pty. Ltd.
4 Lentara Court
Cheltenham, Victoria, 3192 Australia
Email: info@halleonard.com.au

Contents

Frosty the Snow Man

Words and Music by Steve Nelson
and Jack Rollins
Arranged by Eric Baumgartner

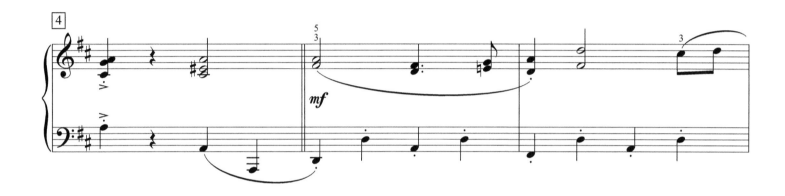

It Must Have Been the Mistletoe
(Our First Christmas)

By Justin Wilde and Doug Konecky
Arranged by Eric Baumgartner

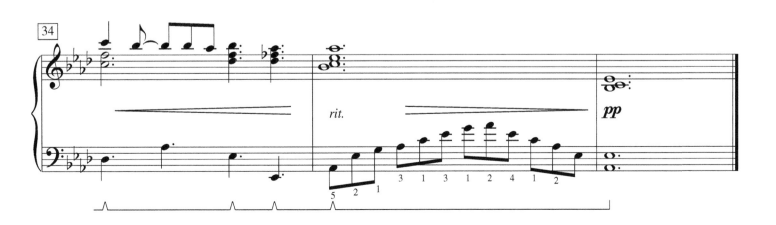

Here Comes Santa Claus
(Right Down Santa Claus Lane)

Words and Music by Gene Autry
and Oakley Haldeman
Arranged by Eric Baumgartner

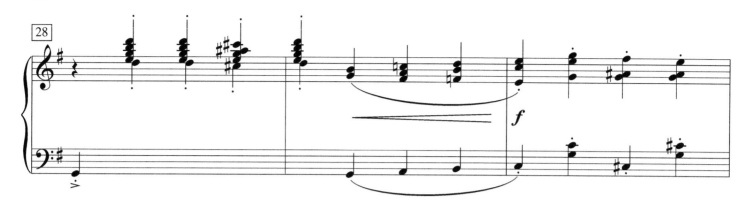

We Need a Little Christmas
from MAME

Music and Lyric by Jerry Herman
Arranged by Eric Baumgartner

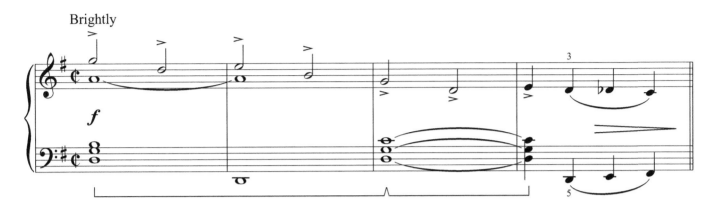

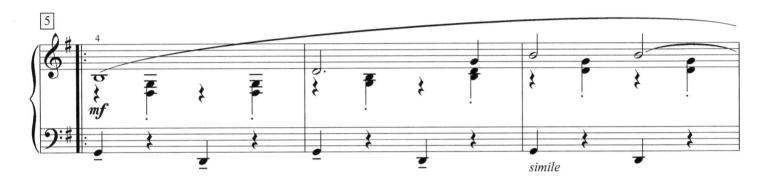

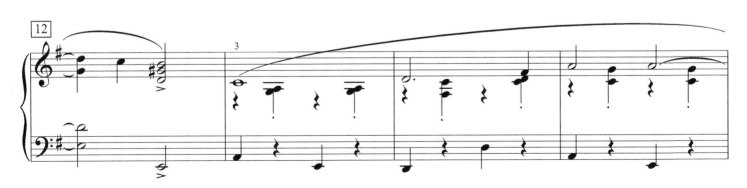

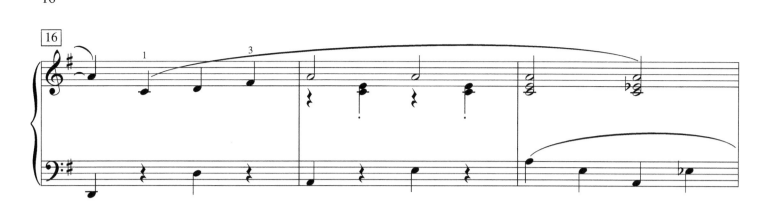

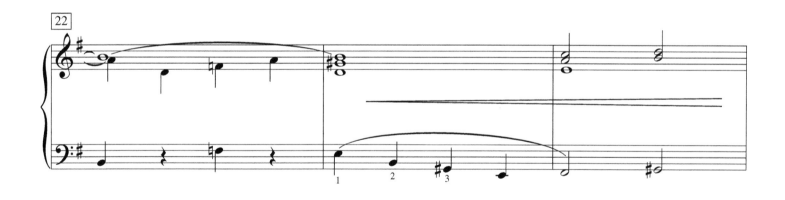

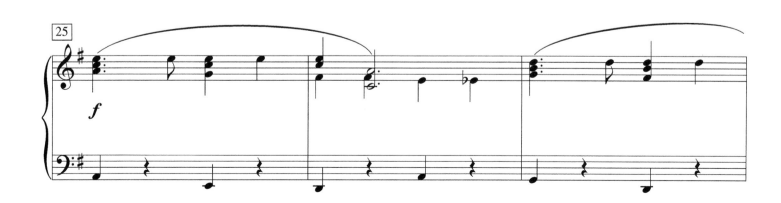

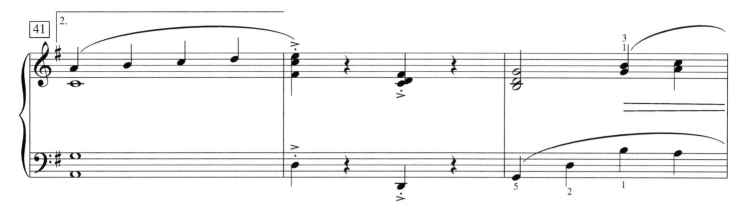

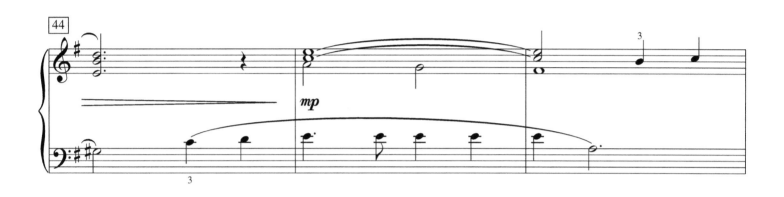

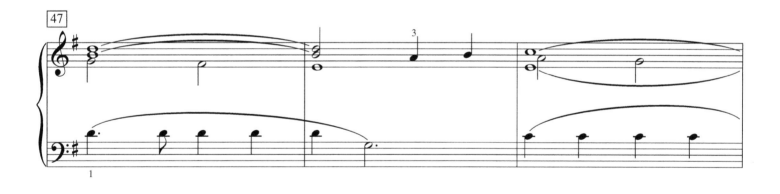

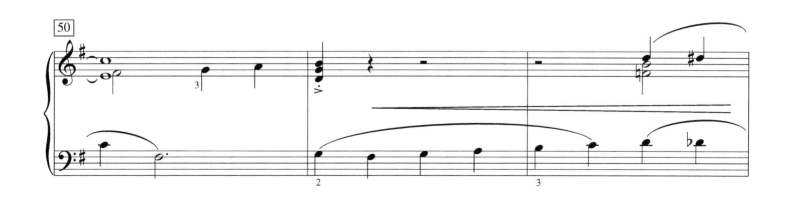

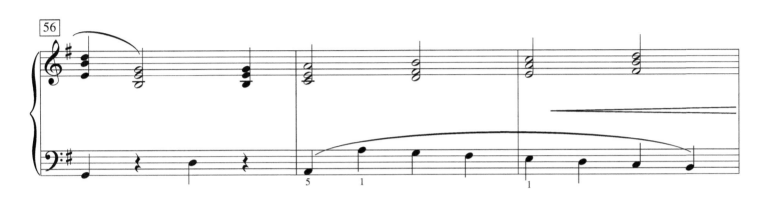

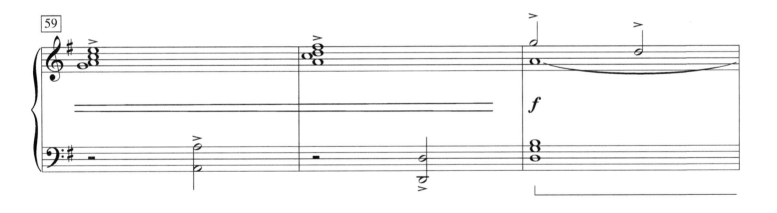

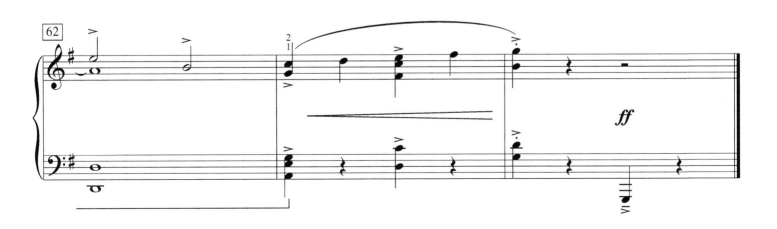

The Christmas Waltz

Words by Sammy Cahn
Music by Jule Styne
Arranged by Eric Baumgartner

Expressively, not too slow

(Everybody's Waitin' For)
The Man with the Bag

Words and Music by Harold Stanley,
Irving Taylor and Dudley Brooks
Arranged by Eric Baumgartner

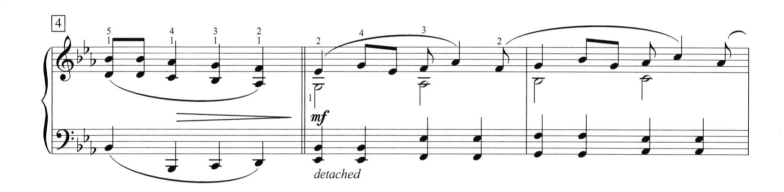

Rudolph the Red-Nosed Reindeer

Music and Lyrics by Johnny Marks
Arranged by Eric Baumgartner

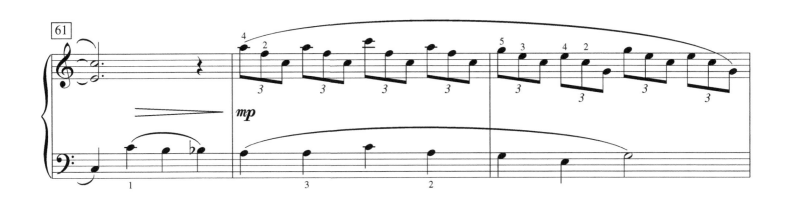

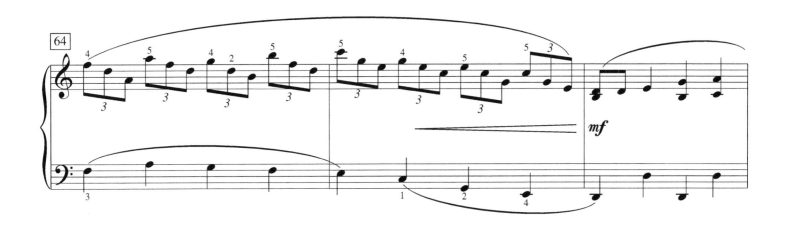

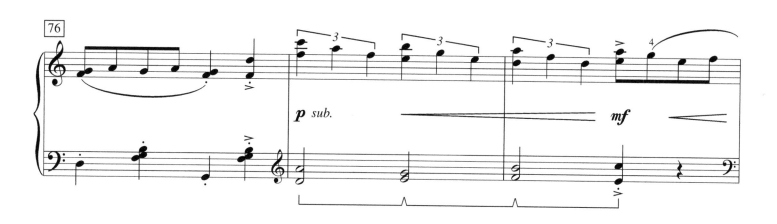

Christmas Time Is Here

from A CHARLIE BROWN CHRISTMAS

Words by Lee Mendelson
Music by Vince Guaraldi
Arranged by Eric Baumgartner

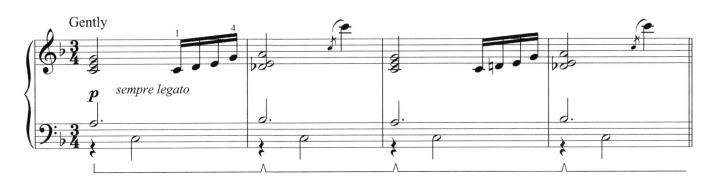

To Coda

D.S. al Coda

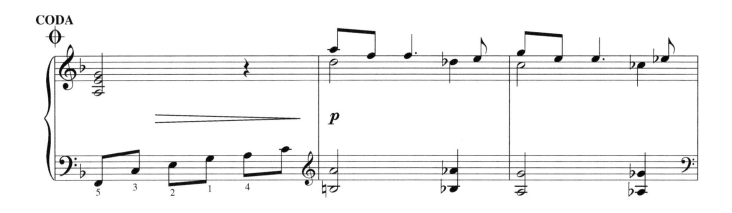

Brazilian Sleigh Bells

By Percy Faith
Arranged by Eric Baumgartner

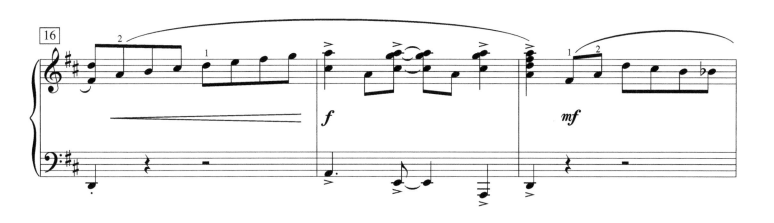

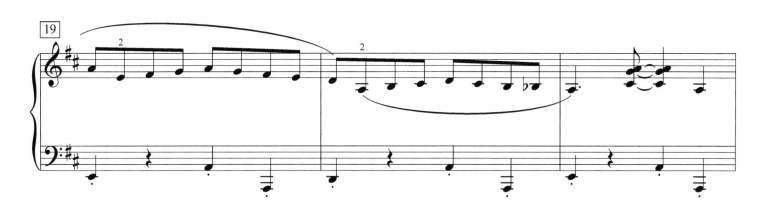

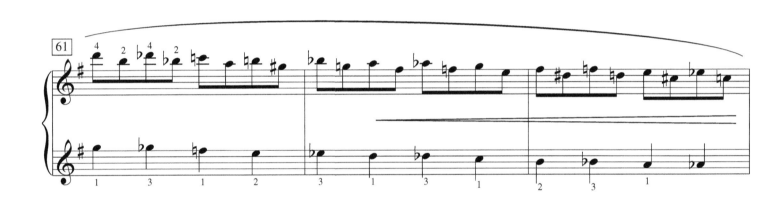

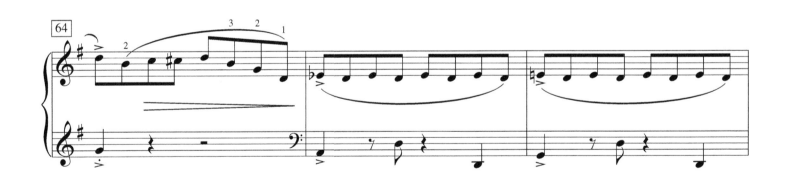

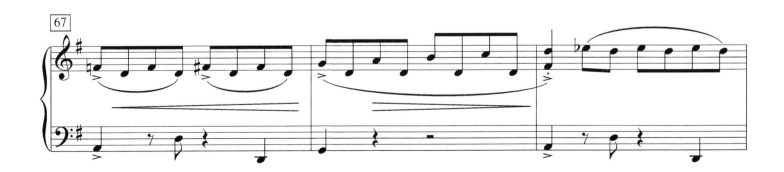

Let It Snow! Let It Snow! Let It Snow!

Words by Sammy Cahn
Music by Jule Styne
Arranged by Eric Baumgartner

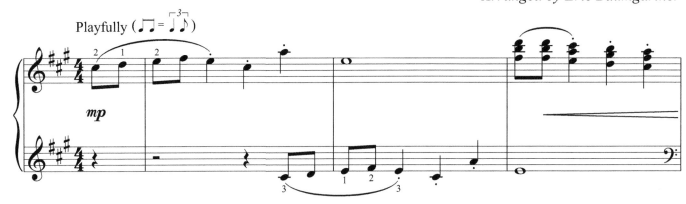

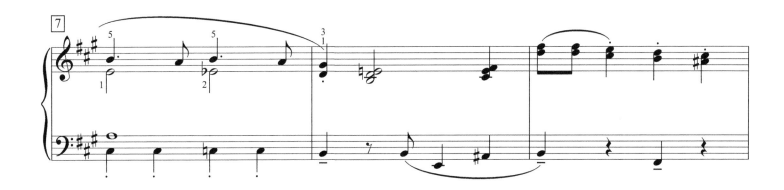

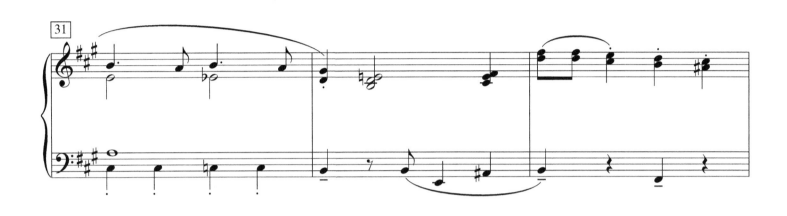

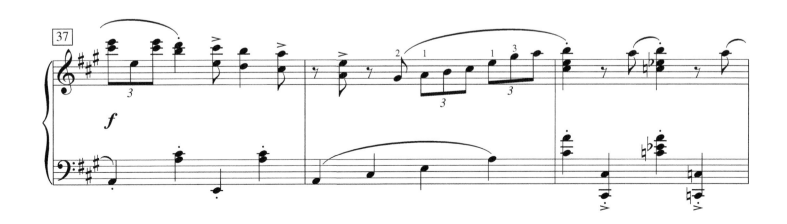

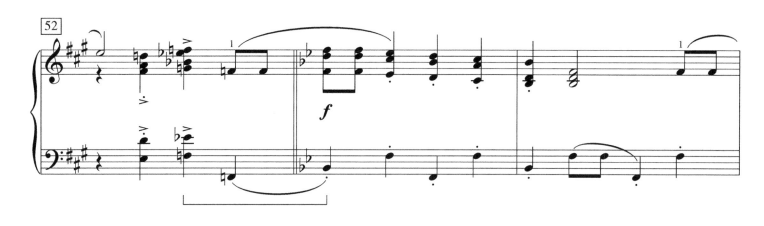

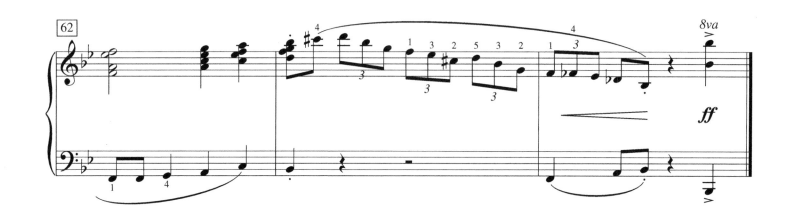